It's Going Down, The Economy, Fool!

Freddie L Sirmans weight losing helpful hint using the "Positive thinking" technique. The definition of the positive thinking technique I'm talking about is: One takes a short saying or quote and repeats it over and over to ones self a minimum of fifty times or more every day. It may take up to six months or more to start feeling any results. This is the quote I use: "I can keep my body slim and healthy through God which strengthens me." Just leave God off or substitute another deity if one doesn't believe in God.

Salt and sodium are the biggest factors in controlling high blood pressure. I buy the gallon jugs of drinking water with 0 sodium. Also, I buy the little squeeze bottles of fresh lemon juice and drink lemon water as my main beverage, no sugar added for me. I believe some water is loaded with sodium for the same reason as processed foods, be aware.

HERE IS WHAT WILL STOP LIBERAL SUICIDE OVER SPENDING

This is a subject I decided to revisit. There is a conservative faction that wants to bring about a states convention to demand the government balance it's annul budget.

On the surface having a convention to do that sounds reasonable and maybe ought to take place. Twenty years ago I probably would have jumped on the bandwagon. However, I have evolved and now realize liberalism has no boundaries or limits to what it will go to keep over spending.

1

It's Going Down, The Economy, Fool!

Today I think any convention of the sort would more than likely cause a total disaster. The first reason is it wouldn't solve the problem. Our welfare state beast is ignoring the constitution and the law now and just adding new laws are not going to make this beast change its ways. The next reason involves human nature.

Liberals tends to be far more intelligent and smarter than conservatives but as a rule are shallow surface dwelling thinkers. The conservative's advantage has always been their focused staying power and deep sound judgment. However, there is a world of difference between today's conservatives and those in the founding fathers days.

Ever since the "New deal" and the come about of our welfare state conservatives has become almost as moral corrupted and shallow minded as liberals. It is a waste of time to pass more laws trying to force liberals to control spending.

They have weak survival instincts and respect no threats in spending from here to kingdom come. But, never forget liberals are not dumb or stupid, when giving up any of their own money they are the stingiest of any group. What it actually boils down to is they struggle with not being selfish to a fault, and that includes spending other people money.

Most conservatives are self-bound by morals and emotional boundaries such as guilt, shame, etc. Where as liberals tends to be far less restricted when going

It's Going Down, The Economy, Fool!

after something they truly want. Nothing that is within the law is going deter a liberal lion/lioness from grabbing power and keeping it.

Power is what this liberal suicide spending is all about. Social spending keeps liberals in power and no amount of morals; love of the country, or anything legal is going to stand in their way of holding on to power. Many liberals tend to be aimless but you give a liberal a cause or a goal and you got an almost unstoppable force on your hand.

If the great USA is to ever get control over suicide over spending from the liberals it can only be done with a physical barrier. So, here we go again, that means repealing the 1938 minimum wage law. Enacting that law is what took away a government-spending barrier in the first place.

That law gave liberals absolute power over private enterprise and private property rights and enable them to tax spend inflate, tax spend inflate, tax spend inflate in a never-ending upward spiral. In fact I don't believe its possible for any free nation to remain free very long with liberalism and liberals at the helm.

Freedom and democracy demands a responsible and self-controlled populace to last over a hundred years in my view. The liberals seized complete control over USA private business enterprise and private property rights with the enacting of the 1938 minimum wage law.

It's Going Down, The Economy, Fool!

Unless that law is repealed this nation will never remain free to 2038 let alone more than a hundred years since the law was enacted.
SIRMANS LOG: 02 APRIL 2015, 2107 HOURS.

CAN THE USA ECONOMY AVOID TOTAL CHAOS IF THE ECONOMY COLLAPSES

I felt like doing some thinking out loud on paper on how much time the country have before our economy totally collapses. I will try to make this article short and not get carried away.

I will start by saying anyone with an ounce of economic wisdom should know that this madness couldn't possibly be sustained. No one knows how or when all of this economic madness is going to finally play out in the end, not even me.

But, I do know two things our welfare state is about to butt heads on. Number one is the days of our welfare state in the role of social and family provider is over, the government just doesn't realize it yet.

The other thing is our welfare state beast will never surrender it power of being a social and family provider even if it means giving up our sovereignty, selling off the country, or whatever to hold on that role.

It is a role the government should never have been in from the start. Government in the role of super provider is like feeding on itself or eating its young.

It's Going Down, The Economy, Fool!

Nature's law of taking the course of least resistance can be extremely disarming and seductive.

That is because no caring and reasonable person wants to see suffering and hardship. But, like drugs, sex, gambling, and anything that gives relief and pleasure, too much of a good thing can be a trap.

While good men and women stood by the shallow minded liberals with good intent eased the government into a permanent role of being a social and family provider. This is a role that for over 6,000 years had always been with the nuclear and extended family head of household.

I'm sure over the centuries governments had tried playing daddy before but before it had always failed. And the only reason it hasn't failed so far in the USA is because of our evil 1938 socialist minimum wage law. That evil law is what has kept this farce going this long.

The evil 1938 minimum wage law has allowed the liberals to grow government unabated by inflating our currency to no end. And they call it growing the economy, which it is not; it is sheer madness and insanity in my view. Sure, this insanity can work for around four generations then it's going to be hell to pay.

That is because ever since this insanity started around 80 years ago it has rotted away the tools and

It's Going Down, The Economy, Fool!

foundation that allows for an organize society to exist. The tools I am referring to are a strong nuclear and extended family system, and an adequate supply of small farmers and home gardeners. That would provide some emergency backup bartering capacity to buy time in case the economy collapses and money was worthless.

In term of long-term survival nothing can take the place of the strong nuclear and extended family system. Without the strong nuclear family system not enough men and women of sound judgment can be produced to maintain an orderly responsible society.

Only the strong nuclear family will make sure proper norms and traditions are instilled in the very young. Experienced wisdom, good morals, and spiritual values must be instilled and passed on or chaos will eventually result.

Sure, living in a world of plenty with full stomachs most of us are so caring with good intentions that we never wake up to smell the coffee. But, I'm here to tell you that we Americans along with much of the industrialized world below the surface are spoiled rotten.

We are comfortable and living in a dream, not knowing that we have almost no tools to survive on when this mad insane economy soon collapses. Without the umbrella of a strong nuclear and extended family system very few are going to make great self-sacrifices for greedy selfish thankless strangers. And self-

It's Going Down, The Economy, Fool!

sacrificing is what it will take to survive as a nation during severe hard and tough times.

However, all of this coming doom can be avoided by repealing the evil 1938 socialist minimum wage law. Even repealing the 1938 minimum wage law is going to cause much pain and hardship but it will be controllable and not turn into chaos.

Once the USA economy is free and unshackled it won't take much to eat and survive, and there is nothing more powerful on earth than a genuine true free market economy. There is no doubt in my mind it will save the USA and western civilization. And may the Gods smile down on this great nation.

P.S. A non minimum wage genuine true free market place economy won't allow inflation and a phony currency for very long, like a liquid a true free market place economy will soon seek its own level.
SIRMANS LOG: 29 MARCH 2015, 0101 HOURS.

THE WORLD WOULD BE A COLD DREARY PLACE WITHOUT LIBERALISM
I'm going to briefly say a few words on liberalism. Sure, I criticize liberalism as much as anyone but I love liberals as well as all people. The world would be a cold dreary existence without liberals and liberalism, who else would guarantee that Bamba is safe and the soft emotional side of life prevails.

However, there has a never been and never will be a

It's Going Down, The Economy, Fool!

society that survives very long with liberalism at the helm. The evil 1938 socialist minimum wage law allowed liberalism to gain control of the USA government. And ever since layer by layer they have been running this great USA ship of state aground.

Liberals have a weak survival instinct and can't see any danger in spending this nation out of existence. They have no concept of the pain, suffering, and turmoil that will result from a collapsed economy due to reckless spending. Plus, on the other hand the liberals have made far too many people government dependent for Republicans to succeed in trying to balance the USA budget.

That approach will surly fail for two main reasons; the first reason is it will definitely create a smaller economy pie, which in the short run will make the economy worse. The second reason is the liberal media and general public is economically ignorant and living in the now and could care less about what is best down the road.

So, when the pie starts getting smaller and painful the Republicans will be booted out of office short order. I think the republicans should just tread water until after November 2016, then do the deed I have been advocating.

Now, I will say again what I have said a thousand times or more, if the republican wants to save this great nation, repeal the evil 1938 socialist minimum wage law, period. That will set free our shackled free

It's Going Down, The Economy, Fool!

market place economy. And there is nothing on earth more powerful than a genuine true free market place economy.

If the republicans set our economy free all they will need to do is be still, the true free economy will take it from there and save this great nation for our children and grand children. However, I'm a realist, I know anything I say, just the opposite will be done, so be it.

In my view there is nothing innate about being a liberal, that is why before our welfare state it was almost unheard of to find a poor liberal. Before our welfare state our poor always had the strongest morals, they could be trusted to work in ones home and very few would take an unborn life.

Today, one poor minority group in the USA are killing the unborn at a higher rate than anywhere in the world. The fact is if any nation is to survive long term Liberalism must never be allowed to completely takeover.

However, there is no denying it; ever since the "New deal" and the 1938 minimum wage law liberalism has dominated the USA government, period. Liberalism, some of it is in the stars but environment always over rules that, which is why I am totally convinced that only repealing the 1938 minimum wage law can break the liberalism death choke hold on this nation.

Liberalism at our helm is like having a kid behind the wheel. Plus, our liberal welfare state has destroyed our culture and morals, but the most deadly of all, it has destroyed our sense of sound judgment. Survival then becomes a far more risky business, sort of like the roll of the dice, or not even dealing with a full deck. **SIRMANS LOG: 26 MARCH 2015, 1414 HOURS.**

THE FOLLY OF THINKING THE USA BUDGET CAN BE BALANCED???
A genuine true non-phony free market place economy without exception must be able to set its own wages and prices, period. The liberals in charge of the government seized that right when they enacted the evil 1938 socialist minimum wage law.

That act castrated the USA economy and has led to the destruction of our culture and morals. And until the USA economy is given back its power by repealing the evil 1938 socialist minimum wage law nothing can break the liberals choke hold on this great nation. Otherwise, there is simply no way this great nation of individual freedom can ever be saved.

Men and women of sound mind with strong survival instincts must give the USA economy back its true power, that way it can save this great nation. Nothing else has the power and discipline to drain this vast liberal swamp and prevent individual freedom from disappearing off the face of the earth forever. God save the USA the last bastion of true individual freedom left in the world today.

The truth of the matter is government is actually a parasite; it can only survive if it has a host to take

It's Going Down, The Economy, Fool!

from. Government is not part of the economy but what it does greatly affects the economy. Every society must have a means of protecting itself from internal and external threats and dangers, and that makes having some form of government a must.

Most governments have the power to take over that is why most private sector host has strong built in protections and total control over the money supply. But, like they say, "The way to hell is paved with good intentions."

On the surface the government doing good and helping people doesn't seem like a threat, and it is not in perspective on a temporary basis. But, in reality government must never become a social and family provider more than on a temporary basis if a free nation is to survive long term.

Whoever is the provider is the boss like it or not. That is why in the USA and Western Europe for all practical purpose the welfare state has taken over. Today there are far too many people dependent on the government to ever put government spending on a diet.

In Western Europe and now in the USA the money priority first goes to the welfare state over the military and all else. And there is only contempt for the profit driven private business enterprise host. Plus, private business days may be numbers because liberal media and the masses don't understand profit and hate it.

Still, there is a savior waiting on a white horse ready to

It's Going Down, The Economy, Fool!

ride in to rescue western civilization. But first, the evil 1938 socialist minimum law must be shot with a silver bullet or a stake driven through its heart by repealing or getting rid of all minimum wage laws entirely. This evil poison pill law must be buried to never rise again for any democracy to ever be safe.

In terms of raw bare boned survival using good intentions and doing the right thing may cause Mother Nature to spit in your face. Just look at the animal kingdom with raw nature, there is no place for good intentions or doing the right thing, except to starve.

Now, you look at the USA economic situation, from a political point of view good intentions and doing the right thing I believe will surely get you booted out of power, period. Folks, let me stop right here and explain, I'm a writer and I write it as I see it. I can be wrong, in fact I hope I am wrong on some of the dire things I see coming down the pike.

I have said it before and am going to say it again, anyone that still thinks the USA and western Europe can be saved as welfare states is economically ignorant in my view. Maybe I'm the one who is ignorant. However, I believe I can dissect and understand the inner workings of an economy as well as anyone.

Yet, for the life of me I can't see any social and family provider welfare state doing anything but slowly devouring its own survival host, which is private business enterprise. Economically, it is just impossible for a welfare state to survive very much longer by

It's Going Down, The Economy, Fool!

constantly dwindling its own only survival host, which is profit driven private business enterprise.

Government can take only so much profit before there is none left to take. Anyone with common sense should know that the USA can't forever reckless spend and keep going deeper and deeper into debt. A reasonable person should conclude that the right thing to do is balance the budget and get your physical house in order.

Sure, that is the responsible thing to do if you are talking about around 80 years ago right after the minimum wage law was enacted. But, today for a political party to take that type of normal responsible action is political suicide.

Now, here is where my super wisdom comes into play. OK, lets just imagine that at the snap of fingers all of the USA debts are paid free and clear, do you think the health of the nation would be solved? My answer would be no! Our debt is a currency problem but civilization existed long before a currency was invented.

The main problems with the USA and western civilization are culture and moral in my view. Contrary to the common view I believe in free nations the economy is the real disciplinarian that actually guards and protects the nations culture and morals.

Sure, we are a nation ruled by law not by man, but I believe the economy is the real power that pulls the strings behind the scene. Also, I believe liberalism is actually what's destroying the USA, which could never have happen with a genuine true free market place economy.

I feel the economy the USA has today is a phony P.... of an economy and has been that way ever since the evil 1938 minimum wage law was enacted. The economy the USA has today doesn't have the power or discipline to protect itself or the nation's culture and morals.

Once the 1938 minimum wage law was enacted, that allowed liberalism a foot in the door to inflate the currency and grow government to no end. Since then the minimum wage law gave government absolute power over prices and wages. Once that happened the aggressive liberals has played to the basic weaknesses in our human nature by promising the moon and back.

The minimum wage law gave government complete control over private property rights and private business enterprise, which it had never had before in the history of the country. By repealing the minimum wage law the economy would regain its power to guard and protect the nations culture and morals, plus boom the economy in real growth not any phony inflated growth like today.

So, the republican think they can take on our welfare state beast and balance the budget, plus remain in power. Well, I'm one that thinks they are in for a very rude awakening. I hope I'm wrong, but I think the beast will defend itself and win. I truly feel only a genuine true free market place economy minus any minimum wage law has the power and ability to take down this beast.

They will never agree with me, but I feel the only wise course the republicans has left to save the USA is to repeal the evil 1938 socialist minimum wage law, "That is all she wrote." As to liberals saving the country, they are the ones hell bent on destroying it and too shallow to even realize it.

SIRMANS LOG: 17 MARCH 2015, 1748 HOURS.

IS THE USA ENTERING A TOTAL BREAKDOWN OF ITS SOCIETY?
You can't get blood out of a turnip. And you can't have a peaceful and orderly society without strong discipline. So, in my view the USA is entering a totally break down of our p.... of a society.

In authoritarian societies brute muscle power and force can be used to maintain discipline. Whereas in free societies people have individual rights and laws that must be obeyed to maintain strong discipline. But, in a free society when there is no brute power and force to maintain discipline two things is a must to prevent a total breakdown of that society.

Those two must things are first a genuine true free market place economy and second a strong nuclear and extended family system. A nations economy trumps everything because everyone must have food and warmth to survive. That is the reason immigration

It's Going Down, The Economy, Fool!

is out of control our welfare state allows our poor and uneducated to avoid doing hot hard work to keep the nation fed.

Somebody gotta do that type work or we all will starve. Now, you try to convince a farmer with his harvest rotting in the field that I'm wrong. Next is the nuclear family, there never has and never will be a society that last very long without a strong nuclear and extended family system.

It is almost impossible to maintain an orderly and peaceful society without making sure the very young are taught proper norms and traditions. That is what happen to the black community, the black man right out of slavery enforced and maintained discipline in the home.

He made sure proper norms and traditions were instilled in the very young before he was kicked out of the home by the welfare state. The welfare state never concerned itself with proper behavior and to this day is still financing its destruction.

Many people are worried about the government completely taking over, well, with the way things are falling apart, the day may come when the people rise up and demand the government take over.
SIRMANS LOG: 12 MARCH 2015, 2229 HOURS.

ABOUT THIS NET NEUTRALITY TROJAN HORSE GIFT
I, great writer Freddie L Sirmans Sr. decided to briefly

It's Going Down, The Economy, Fool!

comment on this "Net Neutrality" thing. The fact is I haven't read hardly anything or listen to very much about it on radio or TV. Still, I decided to weigh in on it anyway.

The truth is what they do don't bother me much one-way or the other. In many ways I feel the world would be better off if the Internet would never have been invented, but its here and anyone standing in the way of progress will get ran over.

I don't need details because I know once the government gets its greed little tax grubbing hands on the throat of the Internet it is ruined forever. It will end up just like our ruined health care system, and screwed up with very few able to afford it.

Before the government seized control of our USA health care system the poor and middle class could pay out of pocket their doctor visits and not over run the nations emergency rooms. Right now, most people don't need the Internet to survive, and the vast majority goes about their daily lives without it. But, once the government seizes enough control over it all of that is going to come to screeching halt.

Our welfare state beast is already slobbering and licking its chops seeing the Internet as a cash cow. They are going to make it where you can't get any kind of health care, a job, or anything else without going on line.

Right now the problem is no one knows how the Internet is going to be taxed, but I assure you the Internet will be made where you can't survive without it or paying to use it.

Warning, I'm fixing to go on a rant and it is my one-man belief and opinion, nothing more. Cease now, or continue reading at your own risk. So, if you want to

It's Going Down, The Economy, Fool!

know what I really think about our future, I may be wrong, but I think the USA will be fortunate if it survive 2015 without a totally economic collapse. And if we survive 2015 this economic lying and insanity can't possibly last much longer.

This is cold hard reality stuff, I just hope they don't start banning or burning my books. I believe that almost everything the USA government puts out concerning our current phony p.... of an economy is propaganda, period. I know beyond a shadow of a doubt that only repealing our evil 1938 socialist minimum wage law entirely can save the USA at this late stage.

Sure, I'm going to be dismissed as a nut case or kook and ignored for now. But, hate me; disagree with me or whatever, I know with my great supernatural wisdom history will prove me right without a doubt. Praise be to God. All of this economic insanity and madness is about to come to a head in my view.

I believe there is an energy or force governing the universe, you can call it God, a superior being, Mother Nature, natural selection, destiny, or whatever, but it maintains a balance in the universe and prevents total disorder.

Every action has a reaction counter part, every positive has a negative counter part, and every good has an evil counter part and vice-versa. Only balance maintains order in the universe. And it affects everything that exists; it is sort of like the whole universe is a unit of one. It is like good and evil is two sides of the same coin.

I will close with this, if you really want to understand and know how an economy and free market place is suppose to work read Freddie L Sirmans Sr. books if you can take it.

It's Going Down, The Economy, Fool!

It saddens me to say this but western civilization has almost become a modern day Sodom and Gomorrah. So, guess what, the universe is beginning to adjust and balance all this same sex marring and mass murdering in the womb with??? You figure it out!!! I know but I will remain mute.

All human emotions evolved to aid human survival in some way. The negative emotions such as evil, hate, etc. are primarily geared to destroy in some way. So, in the eyes of nature there is no such thing as a good or bad emotion they are all just tools in maintaining a balance to keep order in the universe.

I believe when you see evil, evil seemingly like everywhere it is to counter balance something parading as good that is as equal threatening to human survival. My guess is evil is being balanced against the threats to procreation to aid human survival in some way. The process of procreation is in grave danger in the USA and western civilization and Mother Nature is stepping in.

In the USA and Western Europe there is mass means of birth control on demand, mass abortions and killing in the womb on demand, and now we are on a fast path to mass same sex marriages on demand. Now, if you don't think that is a moral and grave threat to procreation and the survival of our species, you are an ignorant fool with a weak survival instinct. Yet, you are the norm, this is what the liberal induced welfare state has brought us to.

Again, disagree if you will, I'm warning you, only removing or repealing the evil socialist minimum wage laws entirely from the USA and western economies can save western civilization from total doom. That is the only thing that can drain this vast liberal swamp. There are just too many two-faced anti-survival monsters dwelling in this self-gratification do-good-er swamp to contend with, the S.O.B. must be drained if the USA is to survive, period.

SIRMANS LOG: 24 FEBRUARY 2015, 1738 HOURS.

THE REALITY OF THE MODERN IMPERIAL USA PRESIDENCY SCROLL DOWN

MEASLES VACCINE DISCUSSION INJECTION: SIRMANS LOG: 05 FEBRUARY 2015, 0020 HOUR
I decided to throw my two cents worth in on this measles vaccine discussion going around: Vitamin B-6 cured my carpal tunnel problems, but the testing science says that is a myth and taking vitamin B-6 had nothing to do with it.

So, when I hear all of these people claiming they noticed the difference right after the vaccine I'm not one to totally dismiss their claims no matter what the supposedly science says. Sure, I believe all vaccines are safe and should be taken.

However, I do have a problem with taking more than one vaccine at a time to save time and labor cost. I think if there is a problem that would be where it lies. I think no vaccine should be give within three months from the last one.

The totally ignored fact is none of this epidemic of diseases would be happening if not for the USA government allowing floods of illegal children in without first being tested or quarantined, Duh.
INJECTION END

I'm going out on a limb and admit to a personal belief. I think the executive branch of government has been allowed to operate out of control ever since the days of

It's Going Down, The Economy, Fool!

Richard M Nixon. Nixon was the first president to go hog wild and start enacting all of these so-called federal environmental laws, safety laws, affirmative action laws, and other such executive only laws.

If the minimum wage law was not destructive enough to a true free market place economy, President Nixon had the gall to even install price controls. But, that was just too extreme and he was soon forced to back off.

Sure, installing these laws was seen as a good thing, but the flaw in allowing one man the power to wield so much power is sooner or later it may lead to rewarding political friends and punishing political enemies. I think we have now arrived to an imperial presidency and there is not a thing politically we the people can do to put a stop to it.

The first thing is we the people don't have the will to stop anything because we as a people are morally and spiritual bankrupt. The second thing is we the people have surrendered our God given family provider role for the most part to a super all powerful welfare state beast. It is a fact whoever is the provider is the boss and you have no choice but to dance to his/her tune.

The almost 200 years before our liberal induced "New deal" hardly anyone was dependent on the government for anything. Sure, as a last resort I feel the government must come to the aid of the people, but never more than on a temporary basis. Right now in a showdown and it may come to that, the states will lose and end up as just federal districts.

The states stupidly voluntarily piss away their real

It's Going Down, The Economy, Fool!

power, now no state governor or legislature appoints and controls its two senators. And, in my view technically speaking United State Senators operate more like independent state agents and are scared to death of special interest groups. Yet, all is not lost.

A genuine true free market place economy is the most powerful thing on earth and will trump even our welfare state beast led by a modern imperial presidency. All the USA need to do to survive is return to a 1937 style economy. The evil 1938 socialist minimum wage law came along and castrated the USA economy.

Any wage or price control destroys a free market place economy's ability to discipline itself, which is its power and greatest asset. So, as you can see only a miracle can save the USA. We have an almost total economically ignorant mass news media and general public to bat that don't know a business can't exist without making a profit, duh.

Most of the world is poor and will always be poor simply because their governments won't allow proprietors to keep more of their profit. I think the USA has two choices in terms of survival, either we repeal or eliminate the 1938 minimum wage law entirely, or hope we survive a total economic collapse, which could be sooner than later.

Folks, I'm a raw crude self-made writer, I know some of my word medicine is bitter to swallow. I say get over it, our survival is at stake, and you can take that

It's Going Down, The Economy, Fool!

to the bank.

Folks, here it is in a nutshell, our nation somehow either gets rid of the evil 1938 socialist minimum wage law or the nation perishes, period.

All of this other stuff I hear everyday like changing the tax system and countless other tinkering here or tinkering there is like nipping at someone's heel or pissing on a barn fire expecting to put it out. Duh.

The conservatives and tea party members are advocating balancing the national budget and cutting out tax wasting social programs. Sure, that would have been wise eighty or so years ago but today it is like spitting into the wind. All that will do is make the beast angrier and the advocates will be booted out of office.

Our welfare state beast now is much too powerful to be brought under control by any such feeble fine-tuning or manipulation today. There is only one force in existence powerful enough to take down this out of control welfare state beast and save the last bastion of true individual freedom left in the world today.

That force is a genuine true free market place economy. But, there exist a huge problem here; a genuine true free market place economy cannot exist if any kind of wage or price control is in place. What the USA has today is a phony P.... of an economy with no power to discipline itself or the county.

No economic discipline is why our culture, morals, and

It's Going Down, The Economy, Fool!

religious structure are shot all to hell. In term of raw survival we have almost no tools left to stay the course. I'm referring to tools like a strong nuclear and extended family system, or enough small farmers and home gardeners for bartering capacity to buy time when this phony economy soon collapses.

The fact is the 1938 federal minimum wage law must be repealed or eliminated entirely before a genuine true free market place economy can save the USA. And the chance of that ever happening seems to be zero to none. So, unless a miracle happens we will just ride out this big phony p.... of an economy until it collapses and sends us all back to the Stone Age.

I predict right now some western nations are searching for the right language to quietly neutralize any wage or price controls. We are on a merry go-round to doom and anyone with an ounce of economic wisdom knows it.

Cut the 1938 minimum wage chain and sic the all power free market place attack dog on this evil tax grubbing welfare state beast, sic-um, sic-um boy.

Ever since the "New deal" the shallow minded liberals and democrats have had this great country by the balls. And there is only one force on earth powerful enough to break their grip. That force is a genuine true free market economy. Otherwise, our greedy tax grubbing welfare state beast is going to finally figure out a way to a seize our guns.

It's Going Down, The Economy, Fool!

And if you don't think at some point our docile humble welfare state beast won't go door to door seizing guns you don't know history. Plus, with today's technology don't ever think they can't find them.

Our armed populace is the last defense saving the last bastion of true individual freedom left in the world today. And our slobbering tax grubbing welfare state beast with an insatiable appetite feels one way or another the guns must go.
SIRMANS LOG: 29 JANUARY 2015, 2048 HOURS

THE OMNIPOTENT POWER OF A GENUINE TRUE FREE MARKET PLACE ECONOMY SCROLL DOWN

INJECTION ABOUT THIS FOOTBALL DEFLATION MADNESS THING: SIRMANS LOG: 23 JANUARY 2015, 1923 HOURS
Obamacare is about to collapse this whole USA economy and the entire national liberal news media's only concern is the weight of a pig skin. Today we have turned into a nation of people with extremely weak to nonexistence survival instincts.

We couldn't recognize a moral or physical threat if it slapped us upside the head. And I blame it all on our liberal induced welfare state. Besides, it shouldn't be that hard to isolate who tampered with the footballs air pressure in the first place.

The first thing is there are cameras all over the place. The second thing is most likely there was always more than one person within sight of the footballs at all times. And the third thing is giving everyone with a reason to be near the footballs a lie detector test.

That being said, I think the whole thing equals making a mountain out of a molehill.

PS: I'm paraphrasing, but, I think it was Vince Lombardi who said, "Winning ain't everything it's the only thing."

INJECTION END

COMING OBAMACARE DESTRUCTION INJECTION: SIRMANS LOG: 23 JANUARY 2015, 1515 HOURS

I THINK BY APRIL 15TH PLUS 30 DAYS WE WILL HEAR THE FIRST RUMBLINGS COMING FROM THE ECONOMIC VOLCANIC ERUPTION THAT MAY LEAD TO A TOTALLY USA ECONOMY COLLAPSE. WE'LL SEE, THE WAIT WON'T BE MUCH LONGER. INJECTION END

IDEOLOGY INJECTION: SIRMANS LOG: 21 JANUARY 2015, 1249 HOURS

I have never in my life advocated for a lower minimum wage because that is even more sinister than a higher minimum wage to the destruction of a true free market place economy. My whole effort on trying to help save the USA and western civilization is repealing or getting rid of any wage or price controls entirely, vamooses.

Getting rid of all shackles and restrictions like any wage or price controls is the only way to let loose the miracle working power of a true free market place economy. That way it will have the discipline and power to kick ass and do whatever it may take to save the USA and western civilization.

Otherwise, western civilization might as well start preparing to be on its knees praying five times a day. The fact is western civilization is going to lose this ideology war not in battle but by actually destroying itself. That being said, all the opposing foe needs to do

It's Going Down, The Economy, Fool!

is just walk in and take over.

Right now in the USA alone when this Obamacare insanity collapses the USA economy we are going to be so busy at each other's throat, hell, I don't know what to expect. All I can do is pray that I'm not losing my cotton-picking mind by letting my imagination get out of control.

Bartender, give me your strongest shot of whiskey, make it a double. There, that should stop any more drift from reality.
INJECTION END

ECONOMIC INJECTION: SIRMANS LOG: 20 JANUARY 2015, 2108 HOURS

USA ECONOMY COLLAPSES DUE TO OBAMACARE, MONEY IS WORTHLESS, NO GOVERNMENT CHECKS FORTHCOMING. NOW, IF YOU THINK THAT CAN'T HAPPEN, THEN YOU'RE A FOOL. YOU DON'T KNOW HISTORY; THERE HAS NEVER BEEN A GOVERNMENT THAT DIDN'T FAIL AT SOME POINT.

I CONSIDER IT A CRIME AGAINST HUMAN SURVIVAL FOR ANY GOVERNMENT TO SEDUCE AND MAKE MILLIONS UPON MILLIONS OF PEOPLE SOLELY DEPENDENT ON ANY SYSTEM OTHER THAN THE NUCLEAR AND EXTENDED FAMILY SYSTEM. CREATING A WELFARE STATE IN THE FIRST PLACE IS JUST PLAIN SOCIETAL SUICIDE.
INJECTION END

It's Going Down, The Economy, Fool!

I see where the USA and Western Europe leadership are brainstorming and scratching their heads on how to solve the immigration problem, the terrorist problem, the economy problem, etc. Well, as a self-made writer I'm fixing to let her rip. I am not about feel good talk and exercises in futility because in terms of sheer survival winning is everything.

There is no sense of me going back over the destruction of what government as a social and family provider along with the welfare state has done to western civilization. It is very simple "We can't have our cake and eat it too."

I think anyone today with an ounce of economic wisdom should know that western civilization cannot and will not survive as welfare states. And anyone that thinks I'm wrong on this is an educated fool. The old folks used to always say, "An educated fool is the worst kind." I'm warning you, one way or another the days of the welfare state is bankrupt and over.

The sooner the USA and Western Europe realizes that fact the better all of our chances of surviving will be. If you mention "Survival instinct" very few today know what the hell you are talking about. Well, I will tell you what I think it is, the harder the struggle in life the greater it is, the least the struggle in life the least it is.

No one has to tell one with a strong survival instinct that there is no bright future for a civilization with same sex marriages, mass murdering in the womb,

It's Going Down, The Economy, Fool!

and birth control galore. Who is going to produce future generations? Duh! No need for me to nag or preach about morals, today very few give a damn anyway, I'm considered to be the nut case and odd man out.

Moral decay and culture rot in western civilization has become too big and overpowering there simply is no possible way for us to survive as a welfare state. The only thing that can possibly save western civilization is a genuine true free market place economy. But, there is an almost insurmountable problem on acquiring a genuine true free market economy.

It can't be done with any kind of minimum wage or price control law in place. That shackles and prevents a free market economy from disciplining itself which is its greatest strength and asset. The minimum wage law must be repealed or eliminated somehow if western civilization is to survive, period.

Of course I expect no one to heed my great wisdom, power never voluntarily concedes anything, and will always go down with the ship first. So, my favorite cake is chocolate, I'll enjoy my big slice now while I can. Who know what tomorrow may bring.
SIRMANS LOG: 17 JANUARY 2015, 2008 HOURS

THIS SEPARATION OF POWERS THING: Scroll down

FEDERAL LAW INJECTION: 16 JANUARY 2015,

It's Going Down, The Economy, Fool!

2111 HOURS

All of these federal bureaucrats making so-called federal law is non-sense, none of it is real law according to the constitution of the United States of America.

All we need is a supreme court to come along with the guts and back-bone to announce that from this day forward all federal laws not passed by congress and signed by the president is null and void, period, (Of course pocket veto's and the sort are exceptions).

Case closed. Of course nothing of the sort is ever going to happen, still, the fact is nothing is supposed to be federal law unless passed by congress and signed by the president, period.

The truth shall set you free, and if nothing more, I feel better just saying it. Smile.
INJECTION END

As a common layman and self-made writer maybe I can explain this separation of powers thing a little clearer. When the founding fathers were setting up our form of government the executive branch of government almost didn't happen.

The first idea was to just have a manager or something of the sort to run the daily operation of government. But, in the end they decided to make it three equal branches of government.

The legislative branch of government would make all

It's Going Down, The Economy, Fool!

laws. The judicial branch of government would interpret and enforce the law according to the USA constitution. And the executive branch of government would carry out the law as written.

However, there seems to be a lot of confusion and misunderstanding concerning presidential executive orders and memos. It really is very simple; the president issuing an executive order is the same as any CEO of a corporation issuing an order or directive to his supervisors and employees.

The president is the commanding chief of the military and head of the executive branch of our government. Eighty or so years ago the president issuing an executive order would mostly affect government agencies and government employees, and had hardly any affect on the vast private sector at all.

That was before the "New deal" when almost no one depended on the government for anything. Well, the hair brained "New Deal" installed act changed all of that. Sure, government must come to the aid of its people but on a temporary basis only.

For government to ever create a permanent class of lifetime dependents is insane. Let's fast forward to today, we live in a welfare state with masses of government social programs and millions upon millions of people solely dependent upon government for survival.

This being the case means any action the government

It's Going Down, The Economy, Fool!

takes is going to affect the private sector almost as much as government agencies and employees.

Still, according to the constitution the separation of government powers is very clear, only the legislative branch of government is entitled to make laws, period.

The executive branch is not entitled to add or take from the law its duty is to carry out the law as written. Don't confuse executive orders with the law.
PS: Another problem concerning the separation of powers is far too many judges are legislating from the bench, too, which is especially true with liberal judges.
SIRMANS LOG: 14 JANUARY 2015, 2228 HOURS

THE USA AND WESTERN EUROPE WILL BE OVER-RUN BY TERRORISM UNLESS THEIR MINIMUM WAGE LAWS ARE ELIMINATED ENTIRELY IN MY VIEW.

CURRENT EVENTS: GREAT WRITER'S THINKING ON THE 2016 USA PRESIDENTIAL ELECTION WINNER:
I think it will boil down to star power and name recognition versus big money. And providing there is not a total USA economic collapse in 2015 I think in a photo finish star power squeaks out a victory.
SIRMANS LOG: 13 JANUARY 2015, 1336 HOURS

INJECTION: 10 JANUARY 2015, 1906 HOURS
Almost everyone think in a free country the government is the most powerful thing, but, that is not necessarily true. I believe ultimately in a free country the economy trumps all. Sure, in terms of raw police and military power the government is all-powerful, but

It's Going Down, The Economy, Fool!

even military power depends on the condition of a nation's economy.

Sure, we are a nation ruled by law, but in the grand scheme of things even the law doesn't have the power of an unshackled and unrestricted free market place economy. What I'm getting at is in a free country ultimately the economy trumps everything.

That is why I keep telling people the evil 1938 socialist minimum wage law de-nuted our economy. That crippled our economy and rendered it weak and helpless to fight off inflation, which our learned economist still calls growth.

That allowed the shallow minded liberals and democrat's to keep superficially expanding our currency enabling them to add social programs and government dependents to no end.

All the while uncle sugar was playing the great super provider daddy role our bread and butter nuclear and extended family units were being destroyed. Uncle sugar was taking away the survival need for a nuclear and extended family unit.

Everything that exists in nature there must be a survival need for it to exist, otherwise it starts ceasing to exist. By uncle sugar taking over as the nuclear family provider, what the hell do you need a nuclear family for, there is no longer a survival need for that, uncle sugar has now taken over that role as the great super provider.

Again, unless our 1938 socialist minimum wage law is eliminated entirely we are a doomed nation in my view, God; I pray that I'm wrong on this.
INJECTION END

It's Going Down, The Economy, Fool!

For a long time I have believed that an economic collapse would eventually doom western civilization. But, with the ever-increasing terrorism around the world I'm not so sure any more. And I will tell you why.

I believe the USA and Western Europe is in denial and unwilling to admit that it is in an all out religious and ideology war. Which, I believe the USA and Western Europe is going to lose unless their minimum wage laws are eliminated entirely.

Western civilization is going to lose this war because of the come about of their socialist welfare state type governments. The come about of the welfare state has made it almost impossible to produce enough men/women of sound judgment and wisdom to protect and safeguard these great nations.

You see, teaching proper norms and traditions to the very young is the only guarantee for maintaining a long-term stable and orderly society. We have failed that must do duty, due to our socialist welfare states we have all be destroyed the nuclear and extended family unit which always faithfully carried out this task since the dawn of history.

Uncle Sugar never made sure the very young was raised properly with the love and discipline to be a productive law abiding citizen that is a must duty of a good provider. A good leader should know that human nature is based on self-interest, logic, and taking the course of least resistance.

That being the case it present the USA and Western Europe with a dilemma that is almost impossible to solve dealing with spending cuts. I'm here to tell you any political party that tries to put a welfare state on a diet is going to run the risk of being chewed up and spit out of power.

It's Going Down, The Economy, Fool!

In fact the USA and Western Europe I'm afraid has created monster socialist welfare state beast's that's going to set modern civilization back to the Stone Age. Another thing western civilization doesn't seem to grasp is the power of repetition in controlling the minds of people.

An example, some religions has mandatory prayers or chants, mandatory repetition locks in a system and it won't change for ten thousand years. That is what western civilization ideology-wise is up against, and unless the USA and Western Europe can find a way to eliminate their minimum wage laws there is not a snowball chance in hell of winning this battle.

The first hurdle is 98 percent of the general public think having a minimum wage law is a good thing. But, anyone with an ounce of economic wisdom will know that the power of a free market place economy is in its discipline, and any wage or price control prevents it from disciplining itself.

Today's USA economy is like a fast runaway train on a suicide mission to hell barreling its way down the tracks with no way to stop or slow it down. This great writer with almost supernatural wisdom is jumping up and down screaming and hollering that the minimum wage engine governor must have malfunction causing the train to speed up and burn out the brakes.

For God sake smash and get rid of the minimum wage engine governor and the trains accelerator will automatic drop back to zero. And in the future stay away from any minimum wage engine governors

Plus, in the USA almost 50 percent of the people will vote for Santa Claus if he promise to keep the checks coming. They feel what the hell does government paying its bills has to do with voting, take the national

It's Going Down, The Economy, Fool!

debt to 50 trillion, what the hell do I care, duh.

I will say this; in terms of raw human survival there is nothing on earth more powerful than an unshackled and unrestricted free market place economy. Take the minimum wage law shackle chains off and then a genuine true free market place economy will win this ideology and religious war. And save western civilization in the process. Nothing else on earth can do it.

Western civilization is suffering from culture rot and moral decay and has become soft and gullible from years of its socialist welfare state forms of government.

I'm telling you, if any government expects to avoid an economic collapse or being over-run by terrorism it better become lean and mean, and soon. And the only way that can be accomplished is to eliminate any minimum wage law entirely, period.

That will create a lean and mean kick ass unshackled and unrestricted economy. Otherwise, political speaking nothing is going to change and we will just keep wondering how long this can last.
SIRMANS LOG: 08 JANUARY 2015, 2048 HOURS

THIS IS A GREAT FABLE THAT YOU MIGHT FIND INTERESTING.

Chapter 1

Once upon a time there was a
Little town called Health-land kingdom,
Located right off the big super MD
Highway leading to the great cure-all
Metropolis. In this town lived
Vitamins, minerals, herbs, humans,

It's Going Down, The Economy, Fool!

And other nutrients.

The town's main goal was to
Keep all of its citizens healthy
Because anyone that   they failed to
Keep healthy would have to face
Terrible traffic jams on the super MD
Highway leading to the great cure-all
Metropolis.

Jim-Niacin (vitamin B-3). Jim-
Niacin doesn't stand alone; he is a
Member of the very powerful B
Vitamin family. In Health-land Jim-
Niacin's job is essential to promote
Life and good health. He regulates
the metabolism and assists in other
Body processes, even though he is
Needed in small amounts compared
to proteins and carbohydrates.

As a coenzyme Jim-Niacin works
to make sure the human body
functions as it should. There are two
major types of vitamins: the water
soluble and the oil soluble. Jim-Niacin belongs to the
water-soluble type vitamins, therefore his doses
must be replaced everyday because
the human body doesn't store his
doses like the oil soluble type.

Since Jim-Niacin is only one
member of the very powerful B
vitamin family he shouldn't work
alone; he should be balanced with
other B vitamin members. Jim-Niacin
is not a bad or evil fellow, but he does
have a bad reputation.

It's Going Down, The Economy, Fool!

Humans are afraid of Jim-Niacin
and rightly so because in too high
doses he may damage the liver, or in
too low doses he does no good. But,
that is not the only reason human
fear Jim-Niacin. Jim-Niacin deals with
circulation and the skin, and he will
heat the skin up like it is on fire and
turn it as red as a beet.

When this happens to a human
for the first time, it will scare some
humans half to death, but don't be put
off, the flushing of the skin is normal
when dealing with Jim-Niacin. It's not
pretty or pleasant but that is how Jim-
Niacin unclogs the capillaries and
small blood vessels throughout the
body.

Captain Fredrico (human). Orry
Fredrico is one of many humans that
Was born and raised in Health-land
Kingdom. Orry Fredrico is a
Carpenter by trade, but as long as he
Could remember he loved the sea.
As a small child he would stand by
The ocean for hours just staring out to
Sea.

As a teenager he would try to
Hop aboard any boat going salt water
Fishing. During his senior year in high
School he went on one of those deep
Sea fishing cruises that goes out for
Four or five hours at a time. On this
Cruises he met Jan Flemmings. Jan
Also loved the sea and they instantly
Became attracted to each other.

It's Going Down, The Economy, Fool!

Within days Jim started dating Jan.

VC (vitamin C). VC also belongs
To the water-soluble type of vitamin.
VC   is truly a heavyweight among
Vitamins. VC is known as a very
Power antioxidant. He is a mighty
Human body protector. He protects
the human body against harmful
effects of pollution.   He helps to
prevent cancer.   He helps to lower
cholesterol and other protection
functions.

Scurvy is a disease that moves
in when there is a deficiency in
vitamin C protection. Years ago,
passengers on ships on long voyages
without fresh fruits and vegetables
had a problem dealing with scurvy.

Jan Flemmings (human). Jan
is a Health-land Kingdom toy
soldier's brat. Just like Captain
Fredrico she has always loved the
sea. She was mostly unanchored
until she met her   soul mate Orry
Fredrico. At first she thought he
loved the sea too much and would not
be a good provider, but his dreamy
bedroom eyes soon won her over.

VE (vitamin E). VE belongs to
the oil soluble type of vitamin. VE is
another mighty antioxidant. VE is
very important in fighting cancer and
cardiovascular disease. Vitamin E is

It's Going Down, The Economy, Fool!

a giant in so many ways. VE is a
natural blood thinner. He promotes
good blood circulation, he promotes
healthy skin, healthy hair, and so
many other healthy body functions.
Vitamin E actually belongs to a
family of eight but falls into two major
groups. These two groups are
tocopherols and tocotrienols. It is the
alpha-tocopherols form that is the
most potent. That is the group VE
belongs to.

John-Pyridoxine (vitamin B-6).
John-Pyridoxine like his cousin Jim-
Niacin is a member of the very
powerful B vitamin family. The fact is
John-Pyridoxine is involved in more
bodily functions than any other single
nutrient. John-Pyridoxine deals with
both the mental and physical health.

He deals with water retention,
sodium and potassium balance, and
fights hard against allergies, arthritis,
asthma, carpal tunnel syndrome, and
on and on. Just like his cousin Jim-
Niacin, John-Pyridoxine shouldn't fight
alone; he should be balanced with
other members of the mighty B
vitamin family.

Mister Disease.   Mister and his
family   showed up one day in
Health-land Kingdom. No one seems
to know where he came from. All
anyone knows is he is mean and evil.
He has no friends and is known to

It's Going Down, The Economy, Fool!

attack humans sometimes without
provocation.

He has no conscience and will
attack anyone that is weak and
helpless. The town and kingdom has
tried to keep him out, but somehow
he always sneaks back in. Our
vitamins, minerals, herbs and others
nutrient citizens have done a good job
fighting him off, but Mister Disease is
a very, very tough customer.

Jim-Niacin and the other nutrient
protectors of Health-land Kingdom
were joyfully patting themselves on
the back because they were doing a
good job protecting the city's
population from Mister Disease and
his cohorts. Jim-Niacin decided to
telephone his cousin John-Pyridoxine.
Jim could hear the phone making its
fourth ring.

"Hello," said John-Pyridoxine.
" This is Jim-Niacin, I decided to
give you a call and touch base on a
matter that I've been tossing around
in my mind lately."
"Tell me about it," said John-
Pyridoxine.

"Well, I've been thinking that all
of the vitamins, minerals, humans,
herbs, and other nutrient citizens
should get together and have a big
town hall meeting. What do you
think."

It's Going Down, The Economy, Fool!

"I think it is a very good idea,"
said john-Pyridoxine.
" Good, then it's a go, I'm going
to start right away making plans,"
said Jim-Niacin. "John you take care
now, I'll talk to you later."
" Bye," said John-Pyridoxine.

Chapter 2

Orry Fredrico and Jan
Flemmings got married after a one
year engagement. Orry got an
associate degree in carpentry from
the local technical college. Twenty
five years later Orry and Jan are now
the parents of a seventeen-year-old
son Rob, and a fifteen-year-old
daughter Melinda.

Almost everyone calls Orry   by
his nickname Captain Fredrico after
he bought his first boat about fifteen
years ago. The boat was a fourteen
footer with a big Mercury motor.
Captain Fredrico now operates his
own contracting business.

It is almost six o'clock p.m. when
Captain Fredrico lets himself in the
carport door which opens directly into
the kitchen. He found his wife Jan
bending over checking her meat loaf
in the oven.

"Hello dear," said Captain
Fredrico in a somewhat tired voice.
" Hello Orry, how did your day
" Pretty good, but my right wrist

It's Going Down, The Economy, Fool!

that's been bothering me the last
couple of weeks seems to be getting
worse, especially at night after I fall
asleep. Sometimes I wake up with a
numb tingling in my right hand. It
feels like somebody is sticking pins in
my hands."

"Orry, I think you need to check
with one of the vitamin citizens. That
sounds like something John-
pyridoxine might be able to help you
with."

"I think you are right dear, I will
give him a call in a few days.

After Marrying Orry, Jan Fredrico
decided to postpone a career of her
own. Becoming a full time housewife
and mother was very fulfilling to Jan.
She even took on the awesome job
of home schooling her kids.

VC (vitamin c) enjoys his job in
Health-land Kingdom taking care of
its citizens. He has a very good
reputation. Humans were using him
probably more than any other vitamin.
Being one of the most powerful
antioxidants, he was in great demand
these days.

In fact, he was being used to
fortify many of today's foods. He
thought the town hall meeting was a
great idea. Why didn't he think of it?
The vitamins and other nutrients were

43

It's Going Down, The Economy, Fool!

doing a good job fighting off Mister
Disease, but he knew that they
couldn't let their guards down, ever.

Just like VC, VE (vitamin E) is
another very powerful antioxidant but
of the oil soluble type. VE is probably
in even greater demand these days
than VC. With so many humans
becoming diabetics these days, VE
with his natural blood thinning power
is a real workhorse. VE is also
looking forward to the big town hall
meeting coming up soon.

On this Monday morning John-
Pyridoxine was kicking back at his
office when the phone ring.
" Hello," said John-Pyridoxine.
" May I speak to John-
Pyridoxine?" said the voice on the
line.

"This is he," said John-Pyridoxine.
" I'm Captain Fredrico and I've
been told you may be able to help me
concerning an ailment. I believe I
have a case of carpal tunnel
syndrome."

"You have the right vitamin,
that is one of my many areas of
expertise."
" Then you will be able to help
me," said Captain Fredrico.

"Hold on a minute, I didn't say
that. Let me explain the situation

It's Going Down, The Economy, Fool!

here, then I can tell you what I may
be able to do. Listen Captain, I'm
going to explain what I do, and it
should take care of your problem, but
then it may not. If I can't cure it, then
I recommend you take the super
MD highway to the cure all
metropolis."

"I understand," said Captain
Fredrico.
" Now, first off," said John-
Pyridoxine, "my maximum dose is
300 mg. per day, that way I will not
damage any nerves. In most cases
100 mg. of my dose will cure the
problem. The golden rule with taking
any nutrients is don't take more than
the recommended dose, because too
much of anything may cause
damage, and never take nutrients on
an empty stomach. So, Captain if
you understood everything I said,
come by as soon as possible. We
have a walk in policy."

"Thank you sir, I should be there
within the hour."

Mister Disease is very upset with
himself for being unable to do more
damage in Health-land Kingdom. He
feels he should be able to bring in
more of his friends like cancer, AIDS,
and even some of his very old friends
like the black plague.

He was getting fed up with those
damn vitamins, minerals, herbs, and

other nutrients. The thing about
those nutrients is they are keeping
him from getting a foothold in Health-
land Kingdom. He feels that if he
could just get a foothold he would be
able to start an epidemic.

Mister Disease decided that he
would just have to work harder.
Sooner or later those humans are
going to think that they are safe and
slack up on utilizing the nutrients.
That is the time he plans to throw his
best punch. He feels that if his friend
AIDS just keeps up the pressure, he
has the best shot at causing an
epidemic.

Most humans don't know Jim-
Niacin and many of those that do
tend to fear and avoid him. As one of
the smallest members of the powerful
B vitamin family, being unknown is
about to change. The reason is Jim-
Niacin along with his cousin John-
Pyridoxine are the ones that called
for and organized the town hall
meeting coming up in a few weeks.
The whole thing was originally
Jim-Niacin's idea.

Since then Jim has
invited the town fathers and secured
all of the permits needed to stage
such an event. Jim has contacted
other town nutrients and humans,
many of them had never heard of
him, or knew who he was.

It's Going Down, The Economy, Fool!

Chapter 3

Captain Fredrico had lived in Health-land Kingdom all of his life and he loved this town. Captain Fredrico got an invitation from Jim-Niacin to attend the town hall meeting coming up in a few weeks.

Captain Fredrico had heard the name Jim-Niacin before and even knew he was a member of the mighty B vitamin family, but that was about all he knew about Jim-Niacin. He didn't know what kind of work or anything else Jim-Niacin did.

Captain Fredrico had heard that the vitamins and other nutrients citizens had become concerned about the health of Health-land Kingdom. The main work our nutrient citizens do is protect our human population from characters like Mister Disease and his friends.

The nutrients knew that cancer and AIDS had almost destroyed a few other towns in the Kingdom. The town hall meeting got Captain Fredrico to thinking. The mayoral election will be coming up in about a year. Captain Fredrico decided that he was going to throw his hat in the ring. Of course he would have to talk it over with his wife Jan first.

After putting in a hard day's work, on his drive home Captain

It's Going Down, The Economy, Fool!

Fredrico thought about the pesky dry
skin that had been plaguing him for
years. It has slowly become more
and more of a problem as time past.

Now it has become a real nuisance.
It has come to the point that he has
to lotion down almost his whole body
every time he takes a shower.
He feels that is unmanly, only
women like to lotion their bodies. He
has tried everything, but to no avail.

He had even got on the crowded
super MD highway and went to the
cure all metropolis, but still to no
avail. At the cure all metropolis all
they did was to prescribe an
extremely expensive body cream that
did little better than over the counter
creams.

He felt truly at his wits end.
There didn't seem to be any hope, he
would just have to accept his
miserable fate. As Captain Fredrico
let himself in the carport door, Jan
was making a salad.
" Hello, dear," said the Captain in
a husky sexy voice.

"Hello, sweetheart," said Jan in
a wooing voice as she dropped
everything and rushed over and
planted a seductive kiss on her
husband's left cheek.

"Now, you go ahead and clean
up, dinner will be ready in a few
minutes. By the way Rob complained

It's Going Down, The Economy, Fool!

about a bout of indigestion after
lunch."

"Did you check with Mr. Blue
Page?" said the Captain.
" Yes, he gave me the names of
several nutrients that work in that
area. The two nutrients that I decided
to use were Stewart-Ginger Root and
Henry-Acidolphilus. Each one of
them gave me heavy doses to give
Rob as needed."

"Good, now let me go ahead
and wash up, then you can tell me all
about it later." After the Captain and
all of the family had sat down to
dinner and the blessing was said, the
Captain revisited the subject of Rob's
indigestion.

"How is your stomach feeling
now, Rob," said the Captain.
" It's fine now, dad, since Mom
had a couple of the nutrients treat it."
" I wasn't sure what to do until
after my talk with Mr. Blue Page,"
said Jan.

"Mr. Blue Page gave me the
names of several nutrients that work
in the area of indigestion. These are
the names that Mr. Blue Page gave
me that deal with indigestion:
Stewart-Ginger Root, Calvin-
Fenugreek, Bonnie-Papaya, Henry-
Acidophilus, and Sammy-Oat bran
tablets.

He also stressed that they did

It's Going Down, The Economy, Fool!

their work with either tablets or
capsules."

"Excuse me for changing the
subject, I have a very important
announcement to make," said the
captain.

"Jan, the mayoral election is
coming up in about a year and I
would like to know if you have any
objections to me throwing my hat into
the ring."

"Gee, I don't know? I've never
thought about being a politician's wife.
Do you think you can win?"
"Dad, I love it, I think it is a great
idea," said Melinda.
"Me too," said Rob.

"I can't guarantee you I will win,
but I believe if I get out there and
shake enough hands I'll have a very
good shot."
" Dad, I'll campaign for you," said
Melinda.

"Honey, If you really want to
run, then count me in as your number
one supporter," said Jan.
"Then it's all settled You are
looking at the next mayor of Health-
land Kingdom."

Ever since John-Pyridoxine had
agreed to help his cousin Jim-Niacin
organize the big town hall meeting
coming up soon, he had stayed busy
calling and talking to the citizens of

It's Going Down, The Economy, Fool!

Health-land Kingdom.

Chapter 4

Mr. Disease was aware of the
big town hall meeting coming up in a
few days, and he definitely was not
pleased about what he was hearing.
The word was they were going to try
to get rid of him. Mr. Disease was
not going to let that deter him, that
had been tried before with his
ancestors all throughout history.

Sure, the discovery of DDT,
penicillin, and modern antibiotics had
given his family some big setbacks,
but some of his old friends like
tuberculosis were beginning to make
a comeback, and the new kid on the
block, AIDS, was really beginning to
raise hell.

Mr. Disease felt that as far as he
was concerned, let them have all of
the town hall meetings they want to, it
was not going to put him out of
business.

Mr. Disease watches the
super MD highway often and as far
as he could tell it was becoming even
more crowded each day. Even at the
big super cure all metropolis they
haven't been able to get rid of his
best friend Mr. Cancer. Mr. Cancer is
still doing an awful lot of damage.

It's Going Down, The Economy, Fool!

On this Monday morning Jan
Fredrico   sure didn't want to battle
the traffic jams on the super MD
highway going to the cure all
metropolis. It was just one of those
days, Her daughter was down with a
cold and she herself was dealing with
a slight kidney infection.

She didn't know? Maybe it was
something she ate that was causing
her back a slight ache in the area of
her kidney. She knew that it would
save her a lot of money and time if
she called Mr. Blue Page and found
out which vitamins, minerals, herbs,
or other nutrients that specialized in
the areas of their ailments.

Jan decided to give the nutrients
twenty-four hours to do their work,
then if there was no obvious
improvement she would get on the
crowded super MD highway to the
cure all metropolis. Jan dialed Mr.
Blue Page. The voice on the line said, " You have
reached Mr. Blue Page
directory."

"Mr. Blue Page, this is Jan
Fredrico.   My daughter has a cold
and my kidneys have a slight ache. I
would like for you to give me the
names of the nutrients that specialize
in the areas of our illness."

"Very well, madam. In the area
of the   kidneys, the association of
VC and Cranberry handle that, and
in the area of colds and flu, the

It's Going Down, The Economy, Fool!

association of Garlic, Echinacea, and
Golden Seal handle that. Will that be
all, madam?"

"Yes sir, and thank you very
much," said Jan. Taking advantage
of their-walk in policy, Jan didn't have
to wait long before she was able to
see VC, the very powerful vitamin C
antioxidant.

"Mrs. Fredrico," said VC, " We
give our doses in mostly tablet form.
I am of the water soluble type, the
body does not store my doses.
Taking too much of my dose is
washed out with the urine. But,
taking too much of my dose also may
cause diarrhea or stomach soreness
in some humans.

Rule number one for dealing with
your kidney problem is to keep
drinking lots of water, then take 2000
mg. of vitamin C tablets three or four
times a day after a meal, also take
2000 mg. of cranberry fruit capsules
three of four times a day after a meal.
That should take care of your
problem, Mrs. Fredrico."

Jan next proceeded to take her
daughter by the association of Garlic,
Echinacea, and Golden Seal to take
care of her cold. After a short wait
Jan and her daughter were lead in to
see Hannah-Garlic.

Hannah-Garlic came from one of
the most powerful and popular of all

It's Going Down, The Economy, Fool!

herb families. Even   the Roman
army would not go into battle without
a member of the garlic family coming
along.

Hannah-Garlic instructed Jan to
give Melinda throat lozenges if
needed, then give her a dose of about
1400 mg. of odor controlled garlic,
three or four times a day after a meal,
also give her a 1500 mg. dose of
combination echinacea-golden seal
three or four times a day after a meal.

"You should see some obvious
improvement in twenty four hours; if
not take the super MD highway to the
cure all metropolis.

"It is also helpful to take heavy
doses of vitamin C after a meal at the
beginning of a cold. But, only at the
beginning of a cold, because if
congestion sets in, vitamin C tends
to make it worse. Warning: Never
take vitamin C or others nutrients on
an empty stomach," she said.
After thoroughly going over
everything, Hannah-Garlic said, "
That is it, Mrs. Fredrico, do you
understand all of my instructions?"

"Yes, Herb Garlic and thank you
very much." While driving home Jan
reminded herself to do her neck
exercises when she got home. It has
been quite awhile since stress has
caused her neck to tense up, but she
Decided that she would go ahead
and do the exercises anyway.

It's Going Down, The Economy, Fool!

Jan believed that feeling stress is
a normal part of life. The better one
learns how to deal with life's
frustrations the better one will be able
to cope with stress. Stress affects
people in many different ways. It
may affect some in physical ways
such as headaches, neck aches,
shoulder aches, etc.

To deal with physical aches it is
helpful to do these exercises. These
exercises are done sitting on the side
of the bed. Sit on the side of the bed
with feet apart flat on the floor for
balance. With both hands rolled into
a fist, place them thumbs inward
down on the bed several inches from
the body on each side.

Start the first exercise by twisting
the neck and entire upper body
counter-clockwise as far as possible,
then twist the neck and entire upper
body clockwise as far as possible.
Do these exercises in sets of one
hundred as many times as one
desires.

Start the second exercise by
leaning the head as far as possible on
the right shoulder, then lean the head
as far as possible on the left
shoulder. Do these exercises in sets
of one hundred as many times as one
desires.

Start the third exercise by
leaning the chin as far as possible

down on the chest, then lift the head
backward as far as possible. Do
these exercises in sets of one
hundred as many times as one
desires.

Chapter 5

On the morning of the big town
hall meeting, Jim-Niacin followed his
daily routine of taking care of the
citizens of Health-land Kingdom. Jim-
Niacin tried to take care of all loose
ends concerning the town hall
meeting by making a lot of last minute
phone calls. He rehearsed the
program with his cousin B-12 who
would be the moderator for tonight's
town hall meeting.

At seven o'clock p.m. sharp Jim-
Niacin arrived at the local high school
gymnasium, the location of tonight's
town hall meeting. The meeting was
scheduled to start at eight o'clock
p.m. There were several satellite
trucks already in place when he
arrived. There were the local radio
and TV crews as well as reporters
from the big super cure all metropolis.

Arriving at the high school was
familiar territory for Captain Fredrico.
He had walked at the high school
track three or more times a week for
several years. The high school track
was a popular walking place for the
citizens of Health-land Kingdom.
Captain Fredrico felt that walking or

It's Going Down, The Economy, Fool!

some type of physical fitness program is a must to maintain good health.

It is a fact that one in good physical condition has almost a ten times better chance of surviving a heart attack, stroke, or any ailment. Also, physical activity plays a big role in controlling diabetes. A big help with diabetes is controlling what one eats. Most humans can control diabetes by cutting way back on starches and sweets and taking a chromium picolinate at each meal.

One needs to eat less meat and include more peas, beans, fresh fruits, and raw vegetables. One needs to include at least one raw fruit or vegetable at each meal because cooking and microwaving food destroys all enzymes and most vitamins.

Enzymes are involved in almost every bodily function, especially the digestive process. Enzymes are mostly divided into two groups: digestive enzymes and metabolic enzymes. The digestive enzymes break down food enabling the body to function properly.

The human body manufactures a limited supply of enzymes, but in order to prevent indigestion and other digestive problems one should get as many enzymes as possible from raw food. Otherwise, the body's limited supply becomes depleted.

It's Going Down, The Economy, Fool!

Jim could see that there was
going to be a very big turnout for
tonight's event. It seemed like his
hard work on getting the word out had
paid off. Several tables were set up
at one end of the gymnasium to try
to accommodate as many as possible
on the big panel of vitamins, minerals,
humans, herbs, and other nutrients.

Everyone were handed a
program as they filed into the
gymnasium.   It read that, "We will not
be able to accommodate everyone
due to the time it would take. The
moderator will ask all questions, but
he will take a few written questions
from the audience." At exactly eight
p.m. sharp B-12 (vitamin B-12)
strode up to the podium.

"Greetings, my fellow vitamins,
minerals, humans, herbs, and other
nutrients, I'm B-12 your moderator for
tonight's town hall meeting," he said.
"First I would like to welcome our
town's fathers, celebrities, and all
other dignitaries to this town hall
meeting. Now, I would like to thank
the vitamin that made it all happen.
He is truly another unsung hero.
Many of you here tonight probably
have never heard of him, but all of
the while he has been out there
everyday doing his job. He is one of
the lesser known members of the
powerful B vitamin family. I am proud
to say this truly unsung hero is my
first cousin Jim-Niacin (vitamin B-3).

It's Going Down, The Economy, Fool!

Stand up, Jim."

"Thank you, thank you, thank
you," said Jim-Niacin as he stood and
the audience loudly applauded.
"Now," said B-12, "before we get
into questions and answers we are
going to let several members on our
panel down here give their name and
vocation. We will start with me. I'm
B-12 (vitamin B-12). One of my
many jobs is to assure proper
digestion and the absorption of food."

"I'm Jane-Ginkgo Biloba. I'm a
very well known herb. I'm mostly
Known for improving memory."
"I'm Sammy-Oat Bran Tablets.
I'm known for my fiber. Fiber does so
many things, for now I will mention
just two, I lower the blood cholesterol
and help stabilize blood sugar."

"I'm Eddie-calcium. I'm a mineral
and I do many things. I'm most
needed for strong bones and teeth
and to help lower blood pressure."
"I'm Mary-Magnesium. I'm a
mineral and of the many things that I
do, enzyme activity is most vital. I
also assist calcium and potassium
uptake."

"I'm Sue-Chromium. I'm a
mineral and of the many things that I
do, maintaining stable blood sugar
levels is most vital."
"I'm VA (vitamin A). I'm a
vitamin and lesser known antioxidant.
My main job is protecting the eyes

It's Going Down, The Economy, Fool!

and some skin problems."
"I'm Dee Dee (vitamin D). I'm a
vitamin, and I'm needed for the
absorption   of calcium and
phosphorus."

"I'm Ned-Zinc. I'm a mineral and
of the many things that I do, keeping
the prostate gland healthy is most
vital."

"I'm Kenny-Saw Pametto. I'm an
herb, my main job is to prevent the
enlargement of the prostate gland."
"I'm Gina-Evening Primrose Oil.
I'm an essential fatty acid. I'm a
necessity that cannot be made by
the human body. I do many things,
but improving the skin is my favorite."

"I'm Patty-Potassium. I'm a
mineral. Of my many jobs I will
name just a few. I help maintain a
healthy nervous system and regulate
heart rhythm, also I help control the
body's water balance."

"I'm Hannah-Garlic. I'm an herb.
I detoxify and protect the body
against infections. I help lower blood
pressure, aid circulation and perform
many other functions."

"I'm Henry-Acidophilus. I'm a
friendly bacteria. My main job is to
aid digestion."

"I'm Bonnie-Papaya. I'm an
herb. I aid digestion. I'm good for
heartburn, indigestion, and bowel

It's Going Down, The Economy, Fool!

disorders."

"I'm Brad-Cranberry Fruit. I'm an
herb. I'm helpful for fighting infections
of the urinary track."

"I'm Stewart-Ginger Root. I'm an
herb. I do many things, but cleaning
the colon, reducing spasms, and
stomach cramps is my favorite."

"I'm Calvin-Fenugreek. I'm good
for the stomach, intestines, eyes,
asthma, sinus, inflammation, and lung
disorders. I also increase sexual
desire."

"I'm Edna-Echinacea. I'm an
herb. I have anti viral properties
and I help boost the immune system.
I'm very helpful against colds and flu."
"I'm Gene-Golden Seal. I'm an
herb. I act as an antibiotic, and have
anti-inflammatory and antibacterial
properties."

I'm David-Dandelion root. I am
an herb. I help cleanse the blood
stream and liver and increase the
production of bile. I'm used as a
diuretic. I help reduce uric acid and
improve functioning of the stomach
and other vital organs.

"That is the last introduction we
will have time for," said B-12. "Now, I
will ask the panel a few written
questions given to me from the
audience, but first let me explain our
role here. Number one is we try to

It's Going Down, The Economy, Fool!

be the first line of defense on
protecting Health-land Kingdom from
Mr. Disease and his cohorts.

"We have some citizens who
don't believe in us and won't use our
services. The next thing is we don't
try to be everything to everybody, our
services and abilities are limited.

We encourage anyone that has doubts or don't believe
in us to take the super
MD highway to the cure all
metropolis. Still, there is a lot we can
do to keep Mr. Disease and his
friends from gaining a foothold here in
Health-land Kingdom.

"Very important: When taking the
super MD highway to the cure all
metropolis, make sure you tell them
which of our services you are
maintaining.

"Now, when I ask a question to
the panel, please let those that
specialize in that particular area of
expertise answer the question. Time
will not allow me to ask but only a few
questions. My first question to the
panel is what can we do to   combat
prostate disease?" he asked.
"I'm Ned-Zinc, and I recommend
50 mg. of zinc per day."

"I'm Larry-Pumpkin Seed Oil, and
I recommend 1000 mg. of pumpkin
seed oil per day."
"I'm Kenny-Saw Pametto, and I
recommend 160 mg. of saw pametto

extract twice per day."
"I'm VE (vitamin E), and I
recommend 1000 I.U. of vitamin E
per day."
"I'm Jim-Niacin, and I
recommend my maintenance dose of
250 mg. of niacin per day."
"Is there anyone else?" said B-
12. "So, that gives us five weapons
to fight prostate disease, and I'm
pretty darn sure that anyone that
arms themselves with these weapons
will be able to keep Mr. prostate
disease away for a very long time, if
not forever. My next question to the
panel is what can we do to deal with
diabetes disease?"

"I'm Sue-Chromium, and I
recommend 200 mg. of chromium
picolinate three times a day at meal
time. I also would like to elaborate a
little on this terrible disease.

"Diet plays a   major role in
controlling this terrible disease.
Everyone with this disease should be
able to home check his blood sugar
level and keep it under control. But,
controlling blood sugar is not the only
problem diabetics face.

"There are problems with the
eyes, blood circulation, and many
others. There is a problem with nerve
damage (neuropathy) especially in
the lower extremities," she concluded.

"I'm VE (vitamin E), and I
recommend 1000 I.U. of vitamin E

per day. Being a natural blood
thinner makes me a great asset to a
diabetic."

"I'm Jim-Niacin, and I
recommend my maintenance dose of
250 mg. of niacin once per day for
one not showing any diabetic
symptoms. On the other hand, for
anyone experiencing the symptoms of
diabetes, especially numbness in the
lower extremities I recommend my
unclogging dose of 250 mg. of niacin
twice per day.

"Too high of a dose of niacin can
cause liver damage and high blood
sugar levels, but too low of a dose
does no good. The 500 mg.
maximum dose per day seems to be
just enough to be effective.

"There have been many lower
extremities cut off because of
diabetes, but I truly believe that if
they had only given Jim-Niacin a
chance I would have saved some of
those limbs."

"Is there anyone else?" said B-
12. "There it is folks, three powerful
weapons to deal with this scourge
diabetes. Now, for the final question
of the evening, the question is what
can we do to prevent extremely dry
skin?"

"I'm Gina-Evening Primrose Oil,
I'm an essential fatty acid and I'm one
of the good oils that the body needs

It's Going Down, The Economy, Fool!

for beautiful skin. I recommend 1000-
3000 mg. of evening primrose oil per
day."

"I'm Jim-Niacin. In my view
problems with dry skin, toe nail
funguses, dandruff, and other skin
problems is almost always a problem
with blood circulation especially in the
capillaries and small blood vessels.

"For extremely dry skin I
recommend my unclogging dose of
250 mg. twice per day after a meal
until the extremely dry skin condition
has been cured, then throttle down to
250 mg. once a day for maintenance.
But, be aware, most humans fear me,
and for good reason, because my
doses are no Sunday picnic or stroll
through the park. My doses may
heat up your skin like it is on fire and
turn it as red as a beet.

"This flushing process is
unpredictable, sometimes it will not
happen at all, then other times it will
last anywhere from five minutes to
thirty minutes. It may not be
pleasant, but it is my only way of
unclogging the capillaries and small
blood vessels," said Jim-Niacin.

"Is there anyone else?" said B-
12. "What more could one ask for;
those were two of the most powerful
remedies that I ever heard of in
dealing with a pesky humiliating dry
skin condition.

It's Going Down, The Economy, Fool!

"Remember, a dry skin problem
is not something to be taken lightly,
because you can see what is
happening to the outer skin, but
what's taking place inside with the
vital organs could be a lot worse.
"Citizens of Health-land
Kingdom, that will end our town hall
meeting for tonight, I would like to
thank everyone for coming. Have a
safe drive home," he said.

Chapter 6

Captain Fredrico was very
impressed with the town hall meeting,
especially learning how to deal with
his long time dry skin problem and toe
nail fungus. It had got to the point
that he hated to take a shower.

It was bad enough struggling
through the warmer months of the
year, but the approach of winter was
almost terrifying because a dry skin
problem becomes much worse during
the winter months. Much of the time
during the winter he had to resort to
what is called a bird bath by washing
only his arm pits and private area.
He had tried all kinds of oils, both
internal and external. He had
traveled on the super MD highway to
the cure all metropolis, but all to no
avail. Since the town hall meeting he
had started off on Jim-Niacin's
unclogging dose of 250 mg. of niacin
twice a day after a meal.

It's Going Down, The Economy, Fool!

The resulting benefits were
obvious within a couple of days.
Within days the treatment was so
effective that the captain could barely
wait to jump into the shower for the
slightest reason. Also, within days
his toe nails had started clearing and
should be completely clear within a
few months.

Also, in a few months the
mayoral election will be taking place.
Captain Fredrico felt very good about
his chances of winning. According
to the latest poll he had a four point
lead.

That night as he and Jan were
setting in the den watching TV,
Captain Fredrico said, "You know,
Jan, if I do become mayor of Health-
land Kingdom I'm going to recognize
Jim-Niacin by declaring a Jim-Niacin
day."

"I know, dear, how much you
love Jim-Niacin. He made it possible
for you to be able to take regular
showers again without you having to
lotion down almost your whole body."
"I don't care how much he is
feared and misunderstood," said the
Captain. "As far as I'm concerned
Jim-Niacin is a miracle vitamin."

"I agree, my darling husband,
about Jim-Niacin's abilities, if humans
would just give him a chance he
would save most of the lower
extremities that are being lost

It's Going Down, The Economy, Fool!

because of Mr. Diabetes Disease."

The Captain got up from his
recliner, walked over to Jan and gave
her a warm tender kiss on her waiting
luscious lips and said, "I'm off to bed,
dear, I'll wait up for you."
"I won't be long, dear," said Jan.

Things had been rather calm in
Health-land Kingdom for the last few
months VC, VE, and John-pyridoxine
all were very busy taking care of the
town's population. About the only
thing going on was the mayoral
election coming up very soon.

They all thought the town hall
meeting did a lot of good for the
community. They felt it educated the
citizens that there was a lot they
could do for themselves concerning
their health care.

That means that one will not
have   to jump on the super MD
highway for the slightest little pin prick
or minor inconvenience. Sure, there
is only so much we vitamins,
minerals, herbs, etc. can do to
promote health, we don't try to be
everything to everybody.
After the town hall meeting Mr.

Disease was steaming mad. He was even thinking of
calling a meeting of all the different diseases. The
nerve
of those vitamins, minerals, humans,

It's Going Down, The Economy, Fool!

herbs and other nutrients trying to get
together and put him and his friends
out of business.

They want to try to put his most
successful friends like cancer,
diabetes, heart disease, and AIDS
out of business. He was not having
it; that was not going to be tolerated.
Mr. Disease started planning.

He would try to attack their left flank
by bringing back some of his old
friends like the Black Plague,
Tuberculosis, and West Nile, next he
would try to rush their right flank with
AIDS to try to split their force, then he
would try to rout them up the middle
with lots of Cancer and Heart
Disease.

I will take no prisoners. Who do
they think this is, this is Mr. Disease
and I don't play, I even quit school
because they had recess. It is on.
How dare they have this town hall
meeting to try and get rid of me and
my friends.

After a long hot summer the day
of the mayoral election had finally
arrived and it looked like it was going
to be a big turn out. At seven o'clock
p.m. Captain Fredrico, Jan, Bob, and
Melinda had comfortable seats at
election headquarters. All of the
election precincts closed at seven
o'clock p.m. sharp.

It's Going Down, The Economy, Fool!

The captain and his family started   watching the tally on the big electronic board as the precincts came in. Captain Fredrico jumped out to an early four point lead and was able to maintain the lead throughout the night as the precincts came in. Then, finally the election supervisor announced, "Citizens of Health-land Kingdom the mayor elect is Orry Fredrico." Within seconds several microphones were thrust in Captain Fredrico's face.

A reporter was almost yelling, "Captain Fredrico, how does it feel being the mayor elect of Health-land Kingdom."

"First, I would like to thank my family and all of the volunteers that worked so hard on my behalf to make this   happen. Next, I would like to thank all of the citizens of Health-land Kingdom who had the faith and trust in me and backed it up by turning out to vote for me.

"Also, I would like to inform those that did not vote for me that I will be mayor of all the citizens of Health-land Kingdom. Finally, I would like to thank my opponent for a good clean hard fought campaign. Thanks again everyone. Good night."

Chapter 7

About one month after Captain

It's Going Down, The Economy, Fool!

Fredrico had been sworn in as mayor
of Health-land Kingdom, he
announced that the first Saturday in
March would be recognized by the
town as Jim-Niacin's day.

On the morning of the first
Saturday in March Mayor Fredrico
stood at the podium at Healthy living
park before a very large crowd.

"Citizens of Health-land
Kingdom, today as your mayor I am
proclaiming today as Jim-Niacin's
day. We have on hand plenty of free
food, drinks, and entertainment. To
kick off this festive day, I'm going to
deliver this short speech about the
vitamin citizen we are celebrating
today.

"Citizens of Health-land, Jim-
Niacin is sort of an enigma. Many
here had never heard of him, and of
those that had, many of them fear
and hate him. Still there is a great
many that love this vitamin to death.

"I myself am one of those that
dearly love Jim-Niacin and the good
work he does. I am not telling you
what I heard about Jim-Niacin, I'm
telling you what I've personally
experienced with my dealing with Jim-
Niacin. I'm giving it to you first hand,
straight from the horse's mouth.

"As I've told my wife and many
others, I don't care what anyone
says, to me Jim-Niacin is a miracle

71

It's Going Down, The Economy, Fool!

vitamin. This small, quiet, lowly
member of the powerful B vitamin
family is a Godsend as far as I'm
concerned. As a proud virile human
male I think of the many, many years
that I suffered with extremely dry
skin.

"For years I tried everything to
get relief from this annoying dry skin
condition. Even at the cure all
metropolis they just prescribed an
extremely expensive body cream that
did little better than cheap over-the-
counter lotions.

"Bathing and warm water had
become the enemy. Washing only
arm pits and the private area was
becoming the norm, and I just hated
my predicament. To me cleanliness
is next to   Godliness.

"Sure, I had heard of Jim-Niacin,
but it was mainly bad stuff, I never
knew about his real power until I
attended the town hall meeting. Over
the years the dry skin problem was
getting worse. Some type of fungus
had invaded my toe nails and my skin
was losing its luster in a few
locations.

"The battle for healthy skin was a
battle I knew I was losing , but no one
could help me and I didn't know what
to do. All of my life I've never been a
quitter, I knew there was an answer,
the problem was finding it, so I just
kept on searching and searching.

It's Going Down, The Economy, Fool!

"I was at my wits end, nothing or
no one seemed able to help me find
relief from my extremely dry skin
condition. Then, at the final hour
when all seemed lost and there was
no hope left, Jim-Niacin came riding
in on a big white horse at the town
hall meeting.

"At the town hall meeting Jim-
Niacin gave out his unclogging dose
of 250 mg. twice a day after a meal.
The first thing is I must warn you that
taking Jim-Niacin's unclogging dose is
no cake walk or stroll through the
park. That is the reason many who
have tried taking Jim's doses don't
like him and is afraid of him.

"When Jim goes to work
unclogging those capillaries and small
blood vessels it is not pleasant by any
means. This flushing process varies
in intensity, sometimes it may be
mild, then at other times your skin
may feel like it is literally on fire.

"This flushing process may last
anywhere from five to thirty minutes,
but seldom lasts more than thirty
minutes. I have no evidence to
support this, but I believe diabetes
itself is caused by a deficiency in
niacin, chromium, and a few other
nutrients.

"Citizens of Health-land I could
go on and on praising Jim-Niacin
because in the past he truly has been

an unsung hero. I will add this and
come to a close. Don't ever go over
his maximum 500 mg. daily dose or it
could cause liver damage.

"In closing, I will assure you that
his unclogging dose got rid of my
dandruff, dry skin, toe nail fungus,
etc. Stand up Jim-Niacin and say a
few words," concluded Captain
Fredrico.

As Jim-Niacin arrived at the
podium he stood tall and proud.
The audience went wild with
applause, then chanted, "We love you
Jim, we love you Jim, we love you
"Thank you, thank you, thank
you," said Jim-Niacin, "and may God
bless this great town and keep it
healthy always."

THE END

A GREAT RESTING SEX POSITION

CHAPTER 1
WEIGHT CONTROL AND HEALTH.
I decided to start this sex technique off
on the subject of weight control and health,
because to be a master lover one's health
and physical condition plays a vital role. I
don't have the answer to losing weight,
probably no one does, that is the reason the
dieting and weight control industry grosses in
billions of dollars each year. Very few people
succeed in keeping excess weight off after
five years.

It's Going Down, The Economy, Fool!

For many of us we have had many,
many years of bad eating habits involving
compulsions that are entwined with our whole
personality. So many times I know that I
have eaten enough and am no longer
hungry, but there seems to be an
overwhelming desire urging me to clean my
plate.

It takes the brain satisfying mechanism
at least 20 minutes to register fully once we
begin eating. Most overweight people have
finished eating two meals by that time.
The mental aspect in losing weight is in
many cases overlooked, so I came up with a
positive thought that gave me some mental
support:

Lose weight without trying.
Anyone familiar with my writing knows
that I have a super strong belief in "positive
thinking" to change behavior. To those that
don't know what positive thinking is, I will
explain. It is a technique to change behavior;
take a phrase or quote and repeats it over
and over to yourself. It doesn't need to be
repeated aloud.
However, to be effective it must be
repeated at least fifty or more times every
day. The more times it is repeated the faster
it will work because it is the repeating
process itself that breaks through to the
subconscious.

An example: Freddie L Sirmans weight losing helpful
hint using the "Positive thinking" technique. The
definition of the positive thinking technique I'm talking
about is: One takes a short saying or quote and
repeats it over and over to ones self a minimum of fifty
times or more every day. It may take up to six months

It's Going Down, The Economy, Fool!

or more to start feeling any results. This is the quote I use: "I can keep my body slim and healthy through God which strengthens me." Just leave God off or substitute another deity if one doesn't believe in God.

Salt and sodium are the biggest factors in controlling high blood pressure. I buy the gallon jugs of drinking water with 0 sodium. Also, I buy the little squeeze bottles of fresh lemon juice and drink lemon water as my main beverage, no sugar added for me. I believe some water is loaded with sodium for the same reason as processed foods, be aware. Just keep saying The quote, God will make a way out of no Way. Mighty forces will eventually come to your aid.

.
Health tip bonus:
A heaping tablespoon full of any leafy vegetable preferable raw mixed with your meal at least twice a day will ease almost all digestive problems.
Another very important factor affecting one's sexual performance is proper nutrition. We all have heard the standard advice, "Eat balanced meals and you won't need vitamins." Sure, that may be true, but most people don't eat properly balanced meals. The fact is very few people consistently eat balanced meals all the time. The last data I read was at least 60 percent of Americans take some type of vitamin.
For myself I am definitely in favor of taking vitamins. I have been taking some type of vitamin for over twenty years.

Everyone is entitled to his own beliefs, but in this day of highly processed foods with many of the natural nutrients lost during processing, and the heavy use of all types of pesticides and herbicides, it stands to reason

It's Going Down, The Economy, Fool!

the body's immune system needs all the
help it can get. I, for one have long believed
cancer to be more of a symptom than a
disease.

There are two main bogeymen that can
get men over forty if they don't stay mentally
and physically healthy. Those two bogeymen
are prostate trouble and impotency. The
biggest cause of impotency in men is from
diabetes, high blood pressure, and certain
types of medication, but the big mean
bogeyman that men truly dread is prostate
cancer.

I don't know what anybody else is
going to do, but to stay sexually healthy
well into old age myself; I make sure I see
an urologist at least once a year.

**PROSTATE DISEASE AND IMPOTENCY
PROTECTION FOR MEN:**
My daily supplements: 50 mg of zinc,
1000 mg of pumpkin seed oil, and 1 capsule
of 160mg of saw palmetto extract twice a
day.

When I do this nobody has to tell me if it
works, I can feel the more intense climax. As
usual, never take vitamins on an empty
stomach. Vitamin supplements are fine, but
nothing takes the place of proper nutrition.
Always eat plenty of fresh vegetables,
plenty of complex carbohydrates, plenty of
fruits, and keep the meats lean and unfried.
Also keep the body physically fit with walking
and exercise. Don't overdo it by trying to do
too much. That is the biggest mistake people
make in staying in shape. When one does

It's Going Down, The Economy, Fool!

too much it becomes very easy to find
excuses to miss a day or a session, then it
stretches into days, soon the individual just
completely quits.

You are a lot more likely to stay with a
brief daily walk for one mile, than to do three
miles once a week. It doesn't take much, but
it must be done regularly.
A brisk one or two mile walk at least
three times a week will do wonders. Another
thing people forget is it is just as important to
stay in shape as it is to lose weight.
Staying in shape will make you feel better
and will save your life.

It is a fact that one who is in shape has
a far better chance of surviving a heart
attack, stroke or any illness than one who is
not in shape. Also it keeps the joints flexible
and helps circulation. So, to hell with losing
weight, just keep walking to stay in shape
and live. Sure, losing weight is cream on the
pudding, but let's stay in shape and live first.

I. THE DIET ASPECT
It helps to have a staple food. Many
people use rice, potatoes, bread, or pasta as
a staple, and serve one or the other almost
every meal. These foods are all starches,
which are fine, but the portions should be
kept small. It's far better to change to one
or a combination of the following foods to
use as a staple, such as peas, green beans,
mushrooms, broccoli, cauliflower, greens,
cabbages, or lettuce, then the portions can
be as large as you like. Fats should be kept
to a minimum.

It's Going Down, The Economy, Fool!

It's best to use oils high in Omega-3
fatty acids such as canola oil, or olive oil.
They reverse the plaque build up in the
arteries. A lot of the vital nutrients are
missing from highly processed foods.
Also, there is wide use of antibiotics and
hormones in the meat raising process, plus
the use of all kinds of pesticides and
herbicides in growing our food.

With this going on our immune system
needs all of the help it can get. Taking
vitamins and mineral supplements is a must
nowadays. Taking vitamins A through E, plus
zinc, calcium, magnesium, and chromium
should be the minimum. Some starches are
needed because they are the body's preferred
source of energy.

A rule of thumb for the hard to lose
weight fighter should be to limit the following
"big 6" foods: rice, potatoes, bread, pasta,
fats, and artificial sweets.
Learn to eat with very little salt. Also,
meats taste just as good seasoned with a
little apple cider vinegar. Obey these rules,
eat 3 or more meals a day and you will lose
weight. Some natural remedies for
indigestion are Acidophilus Capsules, ginger
root tabs, papaya tabs, fenugreek capsules,
and oat bran tablets.

**PROSTATE DISEASE AND IMPOTENCY
PROTECTION FOR MEN:**
Daily supplements, 50 mg of zinc, 1000
mg of pumpkin seed oil, 1 capsules of 160mg
of saw palmetto extract twice a day.

ANOTHER GREAT BENEFIT FOR THOSE OVER WEIGHT TO SEVERELY LIMIT THE BIG 6 FOODS IS:
If one then take 1 or more chromium iodinate tablets daily at meal time it will help control high blood sugar in most people. Also, one should chew his food to a liquid before swallowing, and lastly check with your doctor before trying any weight losing program.

II. THE PHYSICAL ASPECT
Anyone wanting to lose weight needs to first maintain a healthy body, and that can't be done without some type of exercise. It's a fact that someone in good physical condition has as much as ten times a better chance of surviving a heart attack, stroke, or any kind of ailment than someone not in shape.

Almost everyone can take a brisk walk for 25 minutes or more at least 3 times a week. There is no excuse, some type of exercise such as walking, weight lifting, etc. must be done to maintain a healthy body. To keep one's fuel burning (metabolism) rate at its maximum one need to eat 3 regular meals and a snack or two, plus some exercise each day. When one misses a meal the body automatically starts conserving energy and will burn a lot fewer calories.

III. THE MENTAL ASPECT
It's a fact that ninety-five percent of the people that lose weight have regained it all back and more after five years. I believe that is because the mental aspect is almost always ignored.

It's Going Down, The Economy, Fool!

Upon completion most fast eaters will always want more, but if they can just hold off for 10 minutes that desire should be gone.

STRESS RELIEF EXERCISE

Feeling stress is a normal part of life. The better we learn how to deal with life's frustrations the better we will be able to cope with stress. Stress affects people in many different ways. It may affect some in physical ways such as headaches, neck aches, shoulder aches, etc.

To deal with occasional neck aches it is helpful to do these exercises. These exercises are done sitting on the side of a bed. Sit on the side of a bed with feet apart flat on the floor for balance. With both hands palm down several inches from the body on each side.

Start the first exercise by turning the head as far counter clockwise to the left as possible, then turn the head as far clockwise to the right as possible. Do these exercises in sets of fifty as many times as one desire. Start the second exercise by leaning the head as far as possible on the right shoulder, and then lean the head as far as possible on the left shoulder. Do these exercises in sets of fifty as many times as one desire.
Start the third exercise by leaning the chin as far as possible down on the chest, and then lift the head backward as far as possible. Do these exercises in sets of fifty as many times as one desire.

Warning: Always check with your doctor before attempting any exercise program.

CHAPTER 2
SELF CONFIDENCE

Nobody is going to accomplish very much in life unless he has faith in himself. Everyone has a talent for something, and you can do just about anything you set your mind to. The real secret in life is to be willing to try almost anything, no matter what it is. People are different. Some people learn quickly, and others take a lot longer, but everybody can learn, if only they are willing to try.

What is lacking is that many people just don't have the faith that they can do anything they set their minds to. Truly believing in one's self will give one a sense of personal independency. Then one can do for one's self, and not have to depend on other people's good will for survival. The best faith builder I know of is the words, "I can do all things."

All one has to do is say them over and over as a positive thought. Just repeat, "I can do all things through God who strengthen me," at least 50 times each day to one's self. Never quit saying them, because it really doesn't matter whether one believes them or not. It may take six months or longer, but sooner or later the faith will be there. Still, there is the need and will to act, because faith without action doesn't mean anything.

A Great Resting Sex Position:
This is a position where the woman lies on her back and the man lies on his side during

sexual intercourse, Like all things with a little practice one will becomes more comfortable with the position. Now, let the great resting

Resting sex position begin:
To get into the position the woman will take the left side of the bed; she will lie on her back with both legs bent at the knees. From the right side of the bed the man will lay crossways or perpendicular on his back with his groin under her legs that is bent at the knees. Next, the man will lift her right leg, then draw his right knee up to his waist and roll over onto his left side with his right leg between her legs coming to rest on her stomach area or where ever most comfortable.

From this position complete penetration can be achieved with whichever method that is most suitable. This is a very comfortable resting sexual position for both partners that allow all hands free for caressing. This position allows those with low stamina to stop, go, or choose any pace they like. Overall, there is no better position for those that are over weight, those with many health challenges, and those with very little energy.

CHAPTER 3
HOW ANY MAN CAN BECOME A MASTER LOVER WITH THIS POSITION AND TECHNIQUE
I believe being a master lover is an art, not just a skill. I will start this subject by taking a note from a song I once heard. The vocalist went on to say something to this effect, "If we can't get along in the living room the bedroom is off limits". I know there is an exception to any rule, but I don't

It's Going Down, The Economy, Fool!

believe a man can be a great or master lover
unless he can be gentle, kind, and
considerate.

Sure, maybe he can be a good or fair
lover, but not a great or master lover.
Anyone can be a skillful lover because that is
mostly physical, but to make loving an art
one needs to be finely in tune with feelings
and emotions. To be finely in tune with one's
partner's feelings and emotions one certainly
will need to be somewhat considerate, kind,
and gentle.

Certainly one doesn't have to be kind,
gentle, and considerate to make wild
passionate love, or be a "wham-bam thank
you mama" type. You have different strokes
for different folks. Some people are into
kinky sex or anything one can imagine. None
of that is what this pamphlet is about. I feel
95 percent of the subject of sex should be
about love, caring, being considerate, being
committed, and being responsible.

That leaves very little for the physical
act itself. Sure, physical skill matters, but
not nearly as much as most people would like
to think. Mother Nature programmed us so
almost no couple is going to break up for lack
of skill if they have love and consideration for
one another. On the other hand, today's
couples are more skillful than any group in
history, yet we have more divorces and
separations than at anytime in history.
The fault with teaching sex in our public
schools is in most cases they teach it just the
opposite of how it should be taught. I feel if
it is going to be taught; about 95 percent
should be about abstinence, love, caring,

It's Going Down, The Economy, Fool!

being considerate, being committed, and
being responsible. The other five percent
should be about the body, and how to
prevent diseases.

The reason I think being a master lover
is an art is because the first thing a man
needs to learn is every woman is different.
No matter how skillful one is, or what his
technique is, it may not work on a different
partner. Now I will move on to the sexual
position and technique I have selected that
can make any man a master lover.

The position I have selected places the
man on his knees, and he remains in an
upright position, he just doesn't lean forward
like in the missionary position. I think almost
everyone knows that the missionary position
is when the man is on top.

I don't know if it
is really true, but it is said that years ago
when the missionaries first went to Africa, the
only position the Africans had ever known
was from the rear like the animals. So one
night the Africans were peeping in a
missionary couple's bedroom window and saw
the man on top. This was new to them; they
had never seen a man on top. Thereafter the
man on top was known as the missionary
position.

Now I will describe the position I have
advocated. Remember, before intercourse
there should always be several minutes of
foreplay, because it normally takes a woman
a lot longer to get into the proper mood and
provide lubrication. To get into the position
the woman will lie on her back legs apart

It's Going Down, The Economy, Fool!

bent at the knees.

Next, between her legs the man will
assume a position on his knees, with his
knees wide apart for balance. He will keep
his body in a vertical upright position. In that
position the man will obtain complete
penetration to begin intercourse. Once
complete penetration has been established he
should begin using his thumb to manually
manipulate the clitoris.

The first advantage with this position is
the man has both hands free that mean a lot
when one knows what to do. The real goal of
any man is to please his woman. That is the
primary reason a lot of men are into oral sex,
they believe oral sex is the most effective
way to please a woman, but that is not
necessarily true.

What most men don't know is using this
position and technique during intercourse one
can use the thumb to manipulate the clitoris,
and please both himself and his woman at
the same time, far better overall. It is
actually called manual manipulation because
he manually manipulates the clitoris with his
thumb during the act of intercourse, which is
a double whammy. I'm personally against
oral sex, but I realize most people don't feel
as I do.

With Aids and all of the other venereal
diseases going around a condom is a must
nowadays. With this position one can use a
condom and readily please his woman by
safely using the manual manipulation
technique. Another thing about condoms is
when a man hasn't been circumcised there is

It's Going Down, The Economy, Fool!

no loss of pleasure during sex when using a
condom, because the foreskin will still roll
back and forth providing that natural
primitive friction. On the other hand when
one has been circumcised there is no foreskin
to roll back and forth for good friction,
therefore making sex a lot less pleasurable.

Sure, from a sanitary point of view
being circumcised is by far better than not
being circumcised. But I have serious
reservations about automatically having male
babies circumcised at birth.
Circumcision is something a man can
always have done later in life, if he so
desires. That is after he has sowed all of his
wild oats.

By being uncircumcised he will
gladly use a condom because there is no loss
of pleasure while using one during sexual
intercourse. But, on the other hand being
circumcised there is a noticeable loss of
pleasure while using a condom during sexual
intercourse. That is the main reason why
many men hate to use a condom during
sexual intercourse. I'm speaking from
personal experience on this subject, because
I was over age forty when I was circumcised.

Even not using a condom that first year
after being circumcised was filled with regret,
but after the sanitary advantages and the
disappearing of blistering, circumcision finally
won out.
There is one caution about using the
thumb for manual manipulation. It is not as
simple as it may look. Some people are just
naturally good at things, where as it may
take others a lot longer to master the

It's Going Down, The Economy, Fool!

technique. The first thing is one has to learn
how to find the clitoris.

Next he has to realize no matter how
gentle he may be, some women are not going
to like the technique, but their number is
small. One of the latest surveys say that at
least eighty percent of all women require at
least some form of clitoris stimulation to
reach an orgasm.

After the clitoris is located it still takes
skill not to be too rough. The main thing is to
try to keep the area wet and moist. That
should prevent irritation. It helps to
sometime dip the thumb down into the
vagina to help moisten the area. As long as
the area is wet and moist one can use the
thumb in a back and forth, circular or any
motion one desire. But if the area remains
dry, never rub or massage a dry clitoris. In
that case use a gentle press, ease up, press,
and ease up method only.

Here is an additional technique that will
give some women a more intense orgasm,
but as before no matter what the technique
is, it's going to turn off some women. The
technique to give a more intense orgasm will
take some practice to gain experience on how
to judge when one's partner is about to reach
a climax.

So, while manipulating the clitoris
during intercourse, just at the point of the
climax press the thumb down firmly on the
clitoris, at the peak.
Another advantage from this position is
it is perfect for intercourse during pregnancy;
also it is ideal for those that are fat and have

It's Going Down, The Economy, Fool!

big stomachs. For fat people a slight adjustment is
needed. Depending on whether one is right or
left handed, the man simply raises one of the
woman's legs with one arm and uses the
opposite thumb for manual manipulation.
About the only disadvantage for this
position is it places the man on his knees in
an upright position.

That places kissing out of reach, which is very
important for many
couples. Since I'm on the subject of sex,
there are a couple of exercises a woman can
do to make sex much more pleasurable. The
groin area has a couple of muscles a woman
can exercise to learn how to tighten it up.
These exercises go back over thousands of years.

Back in those days the kings had large harems,
and the concubines were in fierce competition
to gain the king's
favor, so those women were the first to
develop these exercises into an art. Any
woman can develop these muscles, all it
takes is practice.
To do the exercise it takes a drawing in,
or sucking-in kind of motion of the
muscles. The first exercise involves the
urinary muscle, just like using the restroom
and stopping in mid stream, draw the
urinary muscle inward, let go, draw it in, let
go, draw it in, let go, in sets of five's a few
times each day.
For the second muscle, do exactly the
same thing except do the exercise using the
bowel muscle. Draw the muscle in, let go,
draw it in, let go, draw it in, let go, in sets of
five's a few times each day.

Always remember something like this is a

It's Going Down, The Economy, Fool!

Completely private matter. No one has to know.
As one exercises these muscles, they
will develop and become very strong. Then
one can tighten and relax from one to the
other of these muscles to create a tight
massage like motion within the vagina.

Lastly, we all have seen the exciting movies
where the man and woman, in a hot rush of
passion, tear one another's clothes off and
make hot passionate love.
That may be fine in the movies or for a
quickie change of pace occasionally, but it is
definitely not the type of lovemaking that
satisfies over 80 percent of the women. A
man should spend at least 15 minutes of
kissing, caressing, and other type of foreplay
before intercourse.

THE END

Freddie L Sirmans Sr.
WEBSITE: FLSirmans.com
You can read excerpts or purchase his books from there.

www.ingramcontent.com/pod-product-compliance
Lightning Source LLC
Chambersburg PA
CBHW072305200526
45168CB00014B/856